Thoughts, Words, Songs of the Heart

Carolyn Myers

WestBow
PRESS
A DIVISION OF THOMAS NELSON

WestBow Press books may be ordered through booksellers or by contacting:

WestBow Press
A Division of Thomas Nelson
1663 Liberty Drive
Bloomington, IN 47403
www.westbowpress.com
1-(866) 928-1240

All Scripture is from the King James Bible translation.

ISBN: 978-1-4908-0315-9 (e)
ISBN: 978-1-4908-0316-6 (sc)

Library of Congress Control Number: 2013913142

Printed in the United States of America.

WestBow Press rev. date: 07/19/13

And it shall come to pass in the last days, says God, that I will pour out of My Spirit on all flesh; your sons and your daughters shall prophesy, your young men shall see visions, your old men shall dream dreams. And on my menservants and on my maidservants I will pour out My Spirit in those days; and they shall prophesy. I will show wonders in heaven above and signs in the earth beneath.

—Acts 2:17–19

Table of Contents

Thoughts

Words

Songs

Preface

As you read, may your spirit be refreshed in the Lord Jesus Christ, and may your cares and burdens be lightened as you learn to give your life to the Master. This little book of my heart was written over a period of years thanks to God's persistent love for me.

A special thanks to my beautiful children, who have all given their hearts to the Lord. As their mother, I have done my best and succeeded in trying to help them find themselves in the only true source of life, Jesus Christ, the Son of the Most High, the Creator and giver of all life.

Above all else, keep your eyes on the eastern skies. The return of our Lord Jesus Christ is very, very close. To Jesus be all the glory and power forever. Come quickly, Lord Jesus. Amen.

Acknowledgments

Special thanks to Apostle Helen and Bishop George Saddler of Into His Chambers Ministries International in Kent, Washington, for their strong love and for their encouragement to continue on and grow in the faith. They have always set an example of excellence in their public and private lives, teaching and preaching the Word without compromise and raising up leaders for the end times. It is an honor to sit under them.

Thanks also to Tracy and Tiffannee for their love and for encouraging me to complete this book. They are such beautiful women of God. They have enriched my life. I know the Lord has great things in store for them. Faithfulness is always rewarded.

Thoughts

A Mother's Heart

Child, I feel you stirring deep within my womb;
You feel like butterflies taking to their wing.

My heart reaches out to touch you with my love;
To think I am honored with you, a gift of life.

It does not really matter if you are a girl or a boy.
You are God's gift to me. O, the untold joy!

I will give you back to Him as you grow beneath my heart,
For all life begins with Him so that is where we will start.

He was the first to give; He has a Father's heart.
I know that I can trust Him to provide loving care.

Even now, my prayers reach upward to touch my Father's throne,
Asking that my life with you will lead you to His home.

Child, I am recalling all the years gone by.
You are now a young woman with children of your own.

I see the Lord fulfilling all I have asked for you.
I am so thankful for His hand of grace.

Child, as you hold your children, see them as He does;
He bought them with His Son; they are His gift to you.

Child, He has called you to be the mother of His children.
Learn to give them back to Him each and every day.

He then will help you as you guide them on life's way.
Know a mother's heart is ever, ever giving
If it has been mastered by the Father's hand.

CAROLYN MYERS

"Before I formed you in the womb, I knew you; before you were born, I sanctified you" (Jer. 1:5).

Resurrection

Lord, so much has been written
About that resurrection day.
As I sit and ponder,
I know not what to say.

So I ask for revelation
That I might impart
New understanding
To the human heart.

Lord, I can see You
In the depths of hell—
The time You spent there,
The victories it entailed.

Lord, how much must man see
Before he bows before You
On quaking, humble knees,
Offering praise and worship?

Thank You for the glory and the beauty
Of what Your love has done.
Oh praise, praise forever
The Father for His Son.

"Jesus said unto her, 'I am the resurrection and the life; he that believeth in me, though he were dead yet shall he live'" (John 11:25).

CAROLYN MYERS

The Fragrance of You

Lord, I love to worship You.
I love the fragrance of You.
I love to come into Your presence
And see You face to face.
Lord, no one can touch me like You do.
There is none like You.
I love the fragrance of You.
I love the glory of You.
With angels all around.
I will worship and bow down.
I will tell You
I love the beauty of You.
When I see You face to face,
I will know I've found my place.
I will worship and bow down.
I will declare the glory of You.
You are majestic to behold
As Your glory unfolds.
You embrace me with Your love.
I can see Your heart
And I know I want a part
In the things You have planned for me.
Lord, I seek Your face,
Knowing You have made a place for me
To be in Your presence.
You are glorious, majestic to behold.
You bought me for a price;
I am not my own.
You have plans for me.
I will worship and bow down.
Lord, I love the beauty of You.

"One thing I have desired of the Lord, that will I seek after; that I may dwell in the house of the Lord all the days of my life, to behold the beauty of the Lord and to inquire in his temple" (Ps. 27:4).

Growing

O Lord, do the people really see
The beauty that belongs to me?

All the things I care about,
All the beauty of living in You?

O Lord, are the people aware
That You see and feel their despair?

Do they know the healing done
When they and their maker are made one?

O Lord, do the people really know?
You give me the glow.

All the things they hope to be
Must begin and end with Thee.

O Lord, what may I do
That I may let them know of You?

All the love and care You give—
You have died that they may live.

O Lord, please help them see
The beauty that belongs to me.

Thank You, Lord, that I may show
The beauty of the ones You grow.

"To appoint unto them that mourn in Zion to give unto them beauty for ashes, the oil of joy for mourning, the garment of praise for the spirit of heaviness; that they might be called trees of righteousness, the planting of the Lord that He might be glorified" (Isa. 61:3).

Carolyn Myers

Jesus

Oh, there is no one
With beauty like Jesus.

He is royal and majestic to see.

Oh, there is no one
As humble as Jesus.

He humbled Himself on Calvary.

Oh, there is no one
With beauty like Jesus.

He is King of Kings, Lord of Lords.

Oh, there is no one
As humble as Jesus.

He shed His blood for you and for me.

At Gethsemane,
Gethsemane,
He bent His knee.

He prayed.
He tarried and bled there.

He asks,
"What will you do for Me?"

"And being in an agony, He prayed more earnestly; and His sweat was as
it were great drops of blood falling down to the ground" (Luke 22:44).

Knowing

I did not know that I walked in darkness
All of my young life.

I did not know that the name of Jesus
Could be a shaft of light.

I did not know that calling on Him
Would start a journey in new life.

I did not know there would be so many choices
I would have to make.

I did not know that knowing Him
Would require my entire life.

I did not know that He loved me,
So He chose to give His life.

I did not know that when He died
He died to give me life.

I did not know; have you been told?
He died to give you eternal life.

"For God so loved the world, he gave his only begotten son that whosoever believeth in Him should not perish but have everlasting life" *(John 3:16).*

Love

Lord, You have loved me against my will;
I had no desire for You,
Yet You loved me still.

Now I desire to do Your will,
For I have learned that my life will never be
All the things I once hoped for me.

In my rebellion,
You did not turn from me.
But with Your love,
You waited patiently.

In Your abounding grace,
I learned of my self-centered vanity;
Vanity, all of my life is vanity.

Lord, I thank You.
Your love has given me hope.
A desire to be Your child,
Serving You with humility.

Lord, Your grace has won.
Your love has captured me.

"Behold for peace I had great bitterness: but thou hast, in love to my soul, delivered it from the pit of corruption: for thou hast cast all my sins behind thy back" (Isa. 38:17).

Prayer

When in prayer you are kneeling,
By faith, you touch His throne.
All who seek Him find Him and never desire to roam.

A feast He is preparing for His chosen few.
Dear one, keep seeking; your prayers are getting through.

If you're in a hurry and wish not to tarry there,
Then you may miss heaven; oh, please do not despair.

As your prayers go upward to His throne of grace,
He, in all His glory, finds pleasure in your face.

If His voice you are not hearing as you kneel in prayer,
Then just seek Him longer—be persistent in your prayer.

His arm of mercy, outstretched a fathom far,
He planned your destiny, He who made each star.

The glory of His face, the pleasures of His hand,
All are yours, dear child; will you take part in His plan?

His Word is your road map.
It points to the gap
And to the man who stood within it: Jesus.
That is the beauty of His plan.

His reward He has promised to the ones who will say yes.
All who seek Him find Him. His loved ones are called blessed.

If, when you are kneeling, you wait and seek His face,
You will find all who seek Him find acceptance in His grace.

"And it came to pass in those days that He went out into a mountain to pray, and continued all night in prayer to God" (Luke 6:12).

"And he went a little further and fell on his face and prayed, saying 'O my Father, if it be possible, let this cup pass from me: nevertheless, not as I will but as thou wilt'" (Matt. 26:39.)

Surrender

All this hurt and pain inside of me.

Seeking, seeking to be free.

Running here and there,

Running everywhere,

Asking questions when I dare.

Never knowing who or what to believe,

Wondering if I've been deceived.

Walking in the darkness when I desire the light,

Never, never winning, I am fatigued from the fight.

Not knowing day from night,

I cry from the depths of me to the Lord of light.

Lord, I surrender.

I give up the fight.

May I take my strength from You

And rest in the warmth of your glorious light.

"Submit yourselves therefore to God. Resist the devil and he will flee from you. Draw nigh to God and he will draw nigh to you. Cleanse your hands, you sinners and purify your hearts, you double-minded" (James 4:7–8).

The King's Highway

The King's highway is not hard to find.
Just follow the road map that's been left behind.
It's that dusty old book left on your shelf.
Once you walk on the King's highway,
You'll find plenty of distractions.
Come this way; go here; go there; over the hill a fair.
Plenty of fun and amusement to delight your sensual side.
In these things, you may even take pride.
Standing in heaven, the King woos His bride.
The one who has been chosen will not stray aside.
She's been bought and paid for at such a great price.
She is determined to be the bride.
They are joined in spirit and they are one.
Though she has never seen Him,
She is determined by learning of Him to smile in His face.
She reads His love letter and she yearns for Him.
She can never be happy without Him, she knows.
Yes, many will fall by the wayside,
Yet onward she goes.
He continually calls to her and whispers His love.
He strengthens and comforts her;
They are married in spirit;
He has conquered her foes.
She has nothing to fear as onward she goes.
He's calling out directions
And prayerfully waiting, for He loves her so.
His voice is calling. If you listen you'll hear.
If you walk on the King's highway,
If you are pure and white,
You are the bride in which He delights.

"And the Spirit and the bride say, Come, and let him that heareth say, Come. And let him that is athirst come. And whosoever will, let him take the water of life freely" (Rev. 22:17).

Water

Giving water to Your little ones
Is something I can do.
Knowing when to give them drink
Would be pleasing unto You.

Sometimes they drink the bitter,
And we must make it sweet.
Giving water to Your little ones
Is a very humbling feat.

Sometimes they will not drink
No matter how we try,
And we know if they do not drink,
They will surely die.

Sometimes they are not thirsty
Because they have gone astray.
So we must lead them back again
To give refreshment to their souls.

Sometimes they want to drink
In excess of their need.
Lord, teaching is not so hard
When we follow where You lead.

Lord, sometimes they are so tired
They get lost along the way.
So we must stop and count the cost
Each and every day.

Giving water to Your little ones
Is something I choose to do.
Knowing that as I give to them
I really give to You.

"Now he that plants and he that waters are one: and every man shall receive his own reward, according to his own labors" (1 Cor. 3:8).

Comfort

Father,
May I comfort one

Who is Yours,
Who has need of care

One who is gentle,
Delicate as angel's hair

One who has been caught and bruised
By Satan's snare

One so delicate,
Who needs Your special care.

Lord, would You use me
To give Your special care?

May I learn
As love I give

I must die
So You can live.

Touch them now,
As love I give.

Restore them, Lord,
So they may live.

"Wherefore comfort yourselves together and edify one another, even as also ye do" (1 Thess. 5:11).

CAROLYN MYERS

Food for Thought

All emotion from without, within,
Where does it all begin?

Does it count emotion from without?
Do all things begin and end with me?

Where am I going?
What are the clues?

Is there something greater beyond me?
What could that greater be?

Will I stop, search, and reach beyond?
What is the purpose of us all?

Is there eternity?

Consider eternity. Where does it begin or end?
Does it end with me?

Quest beyond yourself to the highest Deity.

Pursue it with your life,
For that your prize will be.

Life beyond yourself with the highest Deity.

Will you seek it out or a statistic be?

Venture out beyond the human mind.

There you will find God and eternity.

"But seek ye first the kingdom of God, and his righteousness and all these things shall be added unto you" (Matt. 6:33).

Free

Lord,
What do You want me to be?

I will be humble.
You made me free.
I will be free
To be me in Thee

Lord,
What do You want me to say?

I will be free
To speak it this day.
I will be free
To say it Your way.

Lord,
What do You want me to see?

I will have vision
From You to me.
I will be free
To see as You see.

Lord,
What do you want me to hear?

I will be free
To hear what You say.
I will be free
To obey You this day.

CAROLYN MYERS

"But now being made free from sin, and become servants to God, ye have your fruit unto holiness and the end everlasting life" (Rom. 6:22).

Growing Older

Lord, sometimes I am so sad.
I feel so all alone.

Help me, Lord, to remember
This world is not my home.

I must find the things
You have for me to do

Then endeavor daily
To minister as You do.

I must allow the world to see
Your servitude in me.

Help me to look to You
For all my strength and joy.

To be a humble servant
For whom no job is too small.

So, even as I'm growing older,
May I remember this.

All my problems are nothing, Lord,
When I am found in You.

"The aged women likewise, that they be in behavior as becomes holiness; not false accusers, not given to much wine, teachers of good things" (Titus 2:3).

Carolyn Myers

Jesus' Touch

The gentle touch of Jesus
Is needed everywhere.

I looked within the church.
I could not find it there.

Lord, You must be grieved
To see Your people so barren of Your love.

Help us to remember
Your Spirit is a gentle, gentle dove.

Only when we love
Do we follow Your command.

"Love one another
As I have loved you."

Allow us to die to ourselves
To meet our brothers' needs.

First, though, comes a quiet time
With the healer of mankind, Jesus.

Lord, bring us back to You.
Fill us with Your love.

Jesus, Your touch is needed everywhere.
Touch me, change me
Into the likeness of Your love.
Then I can meet my brother's need.

"For she said within herself, if I may but touch His garment, I shall be whole" (Matt. 9:22).

Life's Way

Child, do you frolic on life's way?
Once you start, do you stop to play?
Do you enter in, then back away?
Do you with zeal start on your way,
Then get off life's path to stop and play?
Do you become engrossed with beauty off the beaten path?
Is there always time to play?
Can't we stop to enjoy beauty along life's way?
Do we run to win or do we forget the pace?
Do we even know we run a race?
Once we start, do we look back?
Is there anyone ahead on the track?
Is there no one behind? Are we all alone?
Do we quit or run by ourselves?
Are there fountains in the park?
Are there stars to light the dark?
Lord, You are the fountain and the light.
Thank You for entering me in the race.
Thank You for running at my pace.
Thank You that I see Your face ever before me as I go.
You always help me attain my goal.
Praise You, Lord, for cool water to drink.
Praise You, Lord, for the heat of the day.
Praise You, Lord, for all things go Your way.
Your hands of grace, Your touch of love.
You sweet Spirit, You gentle dove, I desire Your love.
So if I stop along life's way,
Help me remember when to play,
When to run, to stop, or to rest;
Always to follow in Your footsteps,
To call on Your name, to worship, and to praise You;
To continually look toward my goal.
Thank You Lord, for the life You give.
I give it back for the Master to live.

"Wherefore, seeing we also are compassed about with so great a cloud of witnesses, let us lay aside every weight and the sin which doth so easily beset us and let us run with patience the race that is set before us" (Heb 12:1).

Reaching

Jesus is reaching out
To touch your heart.

Yesterday
He asked someone to pray
For you.

This person did not know you
But still prayed.

That prayer rose up,
Touching the throne of the Father.

Did you feel the prayer?

Did something, anything,
Go right for you today?

Did you know
Your name is written
In the palm
Of His hand?

It's imprinted
By the nail scars.

Yes, Jesus is aware of you.

Today
He asks someone to pray.

"Who is he that condemns? It is Christ that died, yea rather, that is risen again, who is even at the right hand of God, who also makes intercession for us" (Rom. 8:34).

Reflections of the Cross

Son, do you see the reflections of My cross?
All things reflect Me and the things I do for thee.

Take the beauty and splendor of the tree.
Note the rhythmic beauty of the rolling sea,
Keeping time for the creator of eternity.

Do you see the majestic beauty of one lone tree?
Set aside for the crucified,
Carving out in blood His plan for thee,
Grown for the anguish of one man, the Deity.

The One who controls the rhythm of the sea,
The One who chose to hang upon that tree,
Jesus hung there for you and me.
This was all part of things to be.

The crown of thorns upon His head,
The visage marred, the body beat,
The flesh torn, the public scorn.

All the pain of death He chose to bear,
All to reclaim for free our destiny.

Ever so softly, Jesus whispers,
"No, you must not hang upon a tree.
Just take your cross and follow Me."

All these things are reflections of the cross
And the victory of Jesus for you and me.

CAROLYN MYERS

"Looking unto Jesus the author and finisher of our faith; who, for the joy that was set before him endured the cross, despising the shame and is set down at the right hand of the throne of God" (Heb. 12:2).

Talking

Father, as I come before You
To Your throne of grace,
I am so very thankful
There is not a hand of fate.

Knowing how You love me
And that Your best was given,
I know not how to thank You
For this act of love.

Only You, my Father,
Know the depths of me.
All my life's before You.
My heart has been made bare.

I know You will help me
When I feel despair.
Lord, my heart within me
Is hurt and feeling pain.

I do not understand.
Would You please explain?
Father, help me walk in faith
No matter how I feel.

I trust You, Lord and Father,
And desire to walk with You.
Give me strength and hope
To continue on Your way.

Father, I give my all to You,
Knowing it will cost my life.
Father, now receive me.
Replace me with Yourself.

"Shall not God search this out? For He knows the secrets of the heart" *(Ps. 44:21).*

Waiting

Waiting
On the One
Who loves my soul

Waiting
Though the waiting
Takes its toll

I will not be moved
From waiting.
For I have seen a vision
Of what waiting will unfold.

Waiting
In the quiet times

Waiting
Through the storms

Waiting
Is worthwhile
When you are waiting
On the Lord.

"But they that wait upon the Lord shall renew their strength; they shall mount up with wings as eagles; they shall run and not be weary and they shall walk and not faint" (Isa. 40:31).

Wooing

Lord, whisper to me
In the stillness of the night
When my spirit's quiet
And the time is right.

Only You, Lord,
Know the secrets of my heart.
As You look upon me,
Bring all darkness to light.

May Your love
Overshadow any fear I might feel.
My ears need Your touch
To hear Your words to me.

My spirit feels Your wooing
And desires to draw near to Thee.
Keep me, Lord and Master,
In Your tender care.

Shape and mold me
In the likeness of Your love.
Guide me by Your Spirit,
Gentle, holy dove.

Onward, upward in my quest for You.
As I enter into worship,
As I seek Your face,
As I delight in You, change me by Your grace.

"Let us therefore come boldly unto the throne of grace that we may obtain mercy and find grace to help in time of need" (Heb. 4:16)

Change My Heart

I ran from the start
When You asked for my heart,
But You kept Your pursuit of me.

I never gave You a reason.
I never was pleasing,
Never caring about Your heart.

Life's not a game; rules haven't changed.
Life's about living, about freely giving.
You gave Jesus.

I kept on fleeing,
Not really believing Your love was free.
I kept throwing Your love away.

Wounds getting deeper as we drifted apart,
You heard my heart's cry.
You kept Your pursuit of me.

When I fell to my knees,
You answered my heart's cry.
Lord, You changed my heart.

"And I will give them one heart, and I will put a new spirit within you; and I will take the stony heart out of their flesh and will give them a heart of flesh" (Ezek. 11:19)

CAROLYN MYERS

Choices

Life is full of choices,
Every day, decisions made.
Sometimes the price is high
But must be paid.

Sometimes we choose things
That bring hopelessness and despair.
We become burdened with life's cares.
Life just isn't fair.

The sacrifice of Jesus
Gets lost along life's way.

When problems all around
Begin to get me down
And the ground I'm standing on
Begins to shake,
I lift my voice and cry to You.
In faith, I know You hear.

When I listen, I hear You say,
"Choose Me. Choose life.
Choose Me this day.
Tomorrow may be too late."

Lord, when I stand before You,
I want to hear You say,
"Enter in, My faithful servant.
You chose Me; you chose life."

"And if it seem evil unto you to serve the Lord, choose you this day whom you will serve, whether the gods which your fathers served that were on the other side of the flood, or the gods of the Amorites in whose land you dwell; but as for me and my house, we will serve the Lord" (Josh. 23:15).

Life's Target

The target of life is like silver.
It is high in price and value.
Some claim it is a fable.
Others only whisper about it.

It is something that once sampled
Will give you hunger for more.
It is like a vegetable that once eaten
Will give nurture to your body.

It is the sprinkling
Of the blood of Jesus on you.
This will make your heart tender
And quicken your spirit.

It is like a blanket to cover you
From the coldness of life.
It is something that is single.
Only you can do it.

Once this is done, if you grumble about your fate,
A jungle will open in your life.
This will be hard to swallow. You will find yourself
In a tangle set forth by that reptile, Satan.

Only the Father God is our husband.
Only He can make our lives stable.
He is the lantern to light,
The inner candle of our lives.

*"And almost all things are by the law purged with blood; and without
shedding of blood is no remission" (Heb. 9:22).*

Lost

Father, I became lost along the way.
I guess I stopped too long to play.

I looked up and You were gone.
And I thought I was so strong.

Pride raised its ugly head.
I continued on, but I was wrong.

I went my way, unconcerned.
I did not stop or repent.

I did not search; I did not find.
I felt You thought me dead.

Your Spirit in me is crying out.
Lord, You are what life is all about.

Lord, Your Word is true.
There is no life outside of You.

Help me to start anew.
Teach me to live victorious in You.

Thank You, Lord, that You forgive.
Renew my life that I might live.

"The righteous cry and the Lord hears and delivers them out of all their troubles" (Ps. 34:17).

Mercy

If it wasn't for His mercy,
I wonder
Where I would stand?

If it wasn't for His mercy,
I could not
Touch His hand.

If it wasn't for His mercy,

There would be
No grace
In which to stand.

If it wasn't for His mercy,
There would be
No place
For me.

So I will
Praise Him
For His mercy.

By His grace
He set me free.

In His grace
I stand.

"For the Lord is good; His mercy is everlasting; and His truth endures to all generations" (Ps. 100:5).

CAROLYN MYERS

My Lord, My God, My Healer

My Lord, my God,
You heal my heart.

You knew from the start
The times I would fall down.

You picked me up,
Restored my crown.

You whispered
Words of love and encouragement.

You breathed in me
Your breath of life.

You said, "Let's start again."
You said, "I hold all time."

You redeem for me the things I have lost,
Restore to me my destiny.

Gently, You hold my broken heart.
I hear You say, "Tomorrow is another day."

"Today you can start anew."
This I gladly do for Thee.

"My child, destiny is My specialty."

"I have seen his ways, and will heal him: I will lead him also and restore comforts unto him and to his mourners" (Isa. 57:18).

Psalm 23

When we come into the presence of the almighty God,
We bring ourselves in subjection to Him.
He in turn fills us with Himself.
What is in the cup is for us.
The overflow brings healing and deliverance to our brother.
When the Lord anoints our heads with oil,
We have His blessing and become a perfumed fragrance to Him.
He gives us the ability to become fat and rich,
Both spiritually and physically to prosper and be in good health.
When He prepares a table before us in the presence of our Enemies,
Many of us are afraid to sit down to eat, because of fear.
Unless we sit down, eat, and allow the Lord to minister to us,
We will always find ourselves in need.
Since the table is prepared in the presence of our enemies,
The Lord intends for us to partake in their presence.
When we learn to sit down before the Lord
And allow Him to feed us and anoint us
In the presence of our enemies, we have given up fear.
We have surrendered ourselves to the Lord.
He then will give us divine favor.
He will anoint our heads with oil.
Our cup, which has been through the fire,
Will be refined and overflow much more quickly.
Therefore we will be refined.
The heart's motives and intents will be pure.
The overflow will be much greater.
Goodness and mercy shall follow me all the days of my life.
I will dwell in the house of the Lord forever.
Afterthoughts:
Fear no evil; submit yourself to the Lord.
Eat from the table of the Lord in the presence of your enemies.
Receive the anointing of the Lord.

Psalm 23

CAROLYN MYERS

You

Because
You are so special,
And there is only one
Like you,
God finds great joy
When you succeed
At what you do.

Because
Of the beauty
That shines
From only you,
God delights
When you succeed.
His beauty is shining through.

Because
You are so special
I have versed these words for you.

May you always feel
Special joy
When you succeed
At being you.

"Unless thy law had been my delights, I should then have perished in mine affliction" (Ps. 119:92).

The Lamp

I asked the Lord about a spirit-filled life.
He let me see a piece of white linen
With a spot of oil on it.
When I asked Him about it,
He said, "The linen should be soaked with the oil."
I asked, "Wouldn't a linen cloth soaked in oil attract dirt?"
He said, "No, not if given the energy of the Holy Spirit."
I asked the Lord to show me this in a scientific manner.
He gave me the lamp.
He told me many of us are, in the beginning,
Like a piece of white linen. We get only a drop or two of oil,
Then we lie around and collect dirt.
Dirt is attracted to oil; dirt will cling to oil.
Therefore we need to be soaked in oil
And know we are to be a lamp lit and burning.
A linen cloth, with a drop of oil, will attract dirt.
A well-trimmed lamp will repel darkness.
Our lives are like a lamp.
Our wicks, soaked with oil, can when lit
By the fire of the Holy Spirit
Burn for a long period of time,
But only under certain conditions. We must …
1. Know the type and amount of oil to use.
2. Know the amount of the wick to expose to the flame.
3. Know when to allow the fire to burn intensely and when to turn it down.
4. Know when to trim the wick.
5. Keep a good relationship with the supplier of the oil.
6. Keep a good supply of oil on hand at all times.
7. Give care and attention to the condition of the lamp.
8. Never allow ourselves to use cheap oil in place of the original.
9. Go to the manufacturer if we break any parts in normal use.
10. Remember to follow the maker's instructions for best use.

Carolyn Myers

Lead on, Lord God

Lord, Your love flows like a river unto me.

I seek Your face and stand in awe of You,
You who made the heavens.

You, Lord God, give forth
Your love to me.

You give me strength to continue on.

You have freely given healing,
salvation, joy, and peace.

You keep Your eyes on me at all times,
You who never sleep.

You laugh at my successes,
weep at my failures.

I run to You. I fall down.
With gentle hands You lift me up.

I seek Your face,
secure within Your grace.

You call me into the depths of Your Spirit.

Lead on, Lord God.
I choose to follow.

"But without faith it is impossible to please him; for he that cometh to God must believe that He is and that He is a rewarder of them that diligently seek Him" (Heb. 11:6).

Words

Hearken

Hearken, My child,
To the word that is written here.

Hear all that is written.
You have fallen away from Me.

You have no joy.
Know that joy in Me is strength.

Look not to the person
Who writes for Me
And say,
"How can she write?"

I use anyone
I choose.

Return to Me
So that I may bless you.

Prepare yourself for My kingdom.
The hour grows late.

Do not be as the foolish virgins
Who waited for Me but were not prepared.

Yea, I say to you,
You need to prepare yourself for Me.

I return soon.
I bring judgment with Me.

I say again,
Repent and prepare yourself for Me.

CAROLYN MYERS

Come to Me

My daughter, I would say unto you
You are not growing as I would have you grow.
You are not seeking Me as I would have you seek Me.
You have fear; you must come to Me so that I can deliver you from fear.
The more you are intimidated by the Enemy,
The more he will intimidate you.
I call to you. I say to you, "Come."
You waste time; you are lax in worship and praise of Me.
You are lax in reading My Word.
You are lax in your prayer to Me.
Now is the time to stand up and say,
"I will obey God, because He is God."
You may say, "I will do as I wish and God will bless me anyway."
Child, I cannot bless you if you don't obey Me.
You are in My permissive will; I want you in My perfect will.
Will you step into My perfect will, child?
Will you heed and will you obey?
When I call to you, will you answer and say,
"Here am I, Lord; I will do it;
I will obey, no matter what the cost to me"?
My daughter, if you will heed the words that are spoken here,
I will bring My anointing upon you
That you will be able to work for Me
And do the things that I have asked you to do.
Hurry, child, for you have wasted much time.
Time is shorter now than when I called you.
My Son will soon come; there are many things you need to do.
Please be in My perfect will; step out of My permissive will.
Know Me, child, in a way you have not known Me; come to Me now.
I have not called you that I might punish you.
I have called you so that I could heal you.
I have called you so that I could anoint you.
I will not condemn you, child. Come to Me.

Hearken, Child

I desire to bless you.
I desire to grow you,
To have you know Me
In ways that you have never known Me.
Oh child, come in, come in, come in.
Oh child, come in.
You sit idle and you sleep.
My voice speaks, cries out to you.
Awaken, child; awaken, child.
Oh, hearken, child; hearken, child.
Oh, hearken, child; is it a time to sleep?
No, I say.
It is time to awaken, to work.
It is harvest time.
Awaken, get up, and work.
Seek, diligently seek, and study.
Hearken, child, to My voice.
Obedience is so important in this last hour.
Again, child, I say, "Hurry, child."
Time grows so short.
Do you hear My voice when I speak to you?
What am I to do, child, when you heed not?
When you will not listen to My voice?
When you have shut your ears to Me?
Study that you may understand.
Your work for Me is not hard if you love Me.
Child, be obedient to Me.
No matter how small or trivial it may seem,
There is much work to do.
Only when you have yielded will the work be done.
I cry onto you, child, to hearken.
Now, in this time of harvest,
Hearken, child.

Hurry, Child

Why do you hesitate to do My work, child?
Why do you hesitate to do My work, child?
Am I not the Lord God of heaven?
Did I not create all?
Do I not have all power, all strength, to sustain and hold you up?
Did I not say
I would walk with you and be with you
in all you endeavor to do?
Yet you wait, you play games, you hesitate.
You do not seek.
Child, I ask you again to awaken.
Walk into My presence.
Seek Me; love Me.
Give your life to Me that I might set people free,
Release them from their bondage.
Oh child, how can you be so lazy?
How can you have no feelings for the things
I ask you to do?
Return yourself to Me, child, that I may renew you,
That you may be strengthened.
Return unto me, child.
I wait.
I wait, child, with love and forgiveness.
I wait.
Hurry to Me, child.
Oh, hurry to Me, child. I truly forgive.
I love you; I will care for you.
I will strengthen you.
I will lift you up.
Oh child, come to Me.
Come to Me without fear, without reservations.
Hurry, child; hurry, child.
Time grows short.

Look to Me

Look to Me; look to Me.
I your deliverer will be.
Look to Me; look to Me.
I your healer will be.

Look to Me; look to Me.
I your shepherd will be.
Look to Me; look to Me.
I your God will be.

Sing to Me; sing to Me.
I through your song will set you free.
Sing to Me; sing to Me.
I through your song will heal thee.

Sing to Me; sing to Me.
I through your song will lead thee.
Sing to Me; sing to Me.
I through your song will reach to thee.

Worship Me; worship Me.
I through your worship will deliver thee.
Worship Me; worship Me.
I through your worship will heal thee.

Worship Me; worship Me.
I through your worship will lead thee.
Worship Me; worship Me.
I through your worship will your God be.

Master Molder

Joy, My child, joy comes with growth in the Spirit.

I would say to you

If you will walk humbly before Me,

If you will place Me where I ought to be in your life,

If you will commit your life unto Me,

Then I will bring healing unto you,

I will heal you in all matters of your life.

I will heal your marriage.

I will heal you.

I will heal your children.

I cannot do this if I am not your God.

Commit yourself to Me in all your ways.

Allow Me to lead and guide your life,

Give you direction, help you to rise to what I would have you be.

I am the master molder.

I will mold and shape your life as I see fit.

Help in molding your life does not come from man.

Man does not know any of the things I know.

Help is not from man.

Only when you have yielded to Me can I mold and shape you,

Make you a vessel that is worthy to use in My temple,

Holy, sanctified, and set apart by Me to be used for Me.

Yield yourself to Me.

Joy in the presence of My Spirit.

I delight in you, and I desire that you delight yourself in Me.

In Me, there is fullness of joy.

I have all that you will ever need.

Delight yourself in Me that I might give to you what you desperately need.

Let Me fill your cup to overflowing with the sweetness of My Spirit.

I delight Myself in giving to My children

In great abundance.

Come, child. Draw yourself close to Me.

Let us fellowship together,

For I delight in giving pleasure to My children.

Come, child.

My Daughter

My daughter,
You are strong-willed and disobedient.

I will change your heart
Because you have asked Me.

I will open your ears.
You will hear My voice.

I will make you a vessel
Worthy of use.

Prepare yourself, to obey Me.
You will obey.
I have spoken it this day.

Harden not your heart
To My discipline.

My discipline will be much harsher
From this point.

You can no longer afford
To play games.

I am grieved
By your disobedience.

Come to Me.
I will change your heart.

As you make time for Me,
I will change you.

My Son

My son,
Yea, My beloved son,
This night you have received
My greatest blessings
On your life.
Mark this day.
It will be a day to remember,
For now
You have My blessings on the ministry
I have been preparing for you.
You need not fear man.
My anointing is upon you.
You also have My blessing.
Behave yourself in a fitting manner
So that you, like Paul,
May say,
"Follow me as I follow Christ."
Hasten not yourself.
My spirit will always urge you,
Never push or hurry you.
You will walk upon the spiritual sea.
Remember,
Do not be like Peter.
Do not look down.
Keep your eyes on Me.
Remember, Peter asked to come to Me.
I said, "Come."
Your spiritual rope is your faith.
You need not fall into the water.
If you do, remember
Your faith is the rope.
I am the life preserver.
Thank you, son

Singing as You Go

Knowing that the Lord,
Who has called you will be faithful
To fulfill the calling He has placed on your life,
This is the time of purifying for you.
But know that the end product
Will be one of great beauty,
For the Lord is the one who sits,
And with great love
He removes the dross from your life.
Allow your songs of praise to rise to the heavens,
Where the Lord with His listening ear
Will hear and be pleased.
He will draw near to you.
The changes that are coming will be by His hand.
Know that nothing
The Enemy has planned will come to pass.
For the Lord in His love for you
Will keep you.
He will rebuke the Enemy from your life.
He is the Good Shepherd.
You are a young lamb with much beauty.
You have great love for the young ones
The Lord has given you.
They will rise up and bless your name.
Also, because you have kept your love
For the Lord and have not looked elsewhere,
He will give you special honor for your faithfulness.
Know that the hand of the Lord is upon you.
He will remain faithful.
He knows your heart.
He will redeem the time for you.
You will walk upright before the Lord,
Singing as you go.

You Are Chosen

Yea, My son,
Be encouraged in Me.
This day I have called you.

I do not ask you to stand
In your own strength, but Mine.
Many will fall
But I am your strong tower.

I uphold those I choose.
You are chosen.
No one can take you out of My hand.
You do not choose to jump.

Be encouraged.
Praise, sing, and shout.
The Enemy will destroy himself
By confusion.

Shout unto the Lord
With a voice of triumph.
Look up; see Me in My glory.
Is there anywhere I am not?

I AM all.
I AM in all.
Arise, walk, and run.
You shall not grow weary.

Afflictions

My child,
Your afflictions have been many.
You are being refined.
The heat will truly bring all impurities to the surface.
You will then see them and through prayer and fasting
Rid yourself of them.
This is part of your growing process.
You will learn discipline.
Also, learn to know Me.
You will learn of Me through prayer.
You must seek Me daily
To continue growing as I desire you to grow.
Do not get caught up in the things of this world.
Learn to walk in the Spirit.
Fasting will teach your body that your spirit will rule.
Fasting will also help you with prayer.
It will awaken the spirit as the body becomes dead.
This is a process that many never learn,
But to grow in the spirit
And the power of My Spirit,
Fasting and prayer are essential.
I do not grow weary with you.
You are still new but you must learn
To follow the instructions that I give you.
Seek Me first.
The rest of your day will go more smoothly.
Decide now—body, soul, and spirit
Or just spirit.
Hurry, child; again I say hurry.
My love for you is great.
Look to Me.

Come, Child

Oh child, I have given you peace; you are growing in joy.
I am strengthening you each day
As you set forth
To praise and worship Me,
To seek me.
I love you.
I love to hear you praise Me.
You'll find joy in praise.
You'll find healing in praise.
These are things
I desire to give you.
New hope, new life, new meanings, new understandings.
Yes, I want to bless you with fullness and maturity.
Seek and grow.
You are new, but there is much that I desire for you.
Things will be hard at times, but I will give you strength,
Assurance, peace, and joy in abundance.
I find great pleasure in meeting your needs.
Yea, I am your Father.
I desire to hold your hand for assurance
And fill you with joy.
Reach, my child, to Me.
There is no disappointment in your God.
I truly can supply all your needs
Far beyond your expectations.
Come as a little child.
Come hungry to your Father.
Be full with the nourishment of My Word.
I will bless you
And grow you, for I love you much.
There is much to learn and much to do.
Hurry, child.

Covenant

Here is My covenant with you, my child.
I will guard your life and all you entrust to Me.
I will stand for you when you cannot stand.

I will give you joy and peace.
I will supply all your needs.
I will use you.

I will prepare you.
You will be a holy servant for Me.
I will sanctify you and refine you.

Know the purifying fire is hot.
Prepare yourself.
You shall be as fine gold.

More time must be spent
In My Word.
I will open My Word to you.

Be alert.
Learn well.
I will renew
And enlarge My covenant.

Seek me.
I am near.
Enter in.

Psalm 57

Hearing

My child, you need not only feel My Spirit.
You need to hear.
I talk often to My people.
Their ears are shut.
Will you hear Me?
Will you obey?

I am looking for people to hear and obey.
If you will fast and seek My face,
I will move and strengthen you
And bring you to a place where you will obey.
Call to me in a loud voice.
Call until I answer you.
Call day and night.
Pray continually.

There is much work to do
But little time left to work.
You will bring many people to Me through your obedience.
Come now.
Enter into a deeper walk with Me.
Hasten yourself; deny yourself.
Follow Me.
I am the giver of eternal life.

My daughter,
I have looked down upon you this day.
You have found favor in My sight.
Continue to seek Me.
I will move mightily in your life.
Learn to work with Me and for Me.
Allow Me to teach you.

Isaiah 49

I have called you with your eyes open.
I have not hidden anything from you.
I have given you many choices.
You have the right to know
That your decisions are not based on fear.

I have called you and anointed you
To be a servant unto Me.
You have chosen to be thus.

I have many things for you to do.
The humbleness of your spirit
Is pleasing in My sight.

Yea, you have been walking in disobedience.
You have fallen by the wayside.

I have not left you there.
I have followed after you.
I have poured in the oil and the wine.

I have caused
The wind of My Spirit
To be blown into you,
Giving you back the life
You have been careless with.

From this day forth, you will walk
In obedience before Me.

The calling that I have placed upon you
Will be stronger than before; it will overcome you.
You will no longer walk in defeat.
You will be established for My namesake.

My Gift

My child, I see the sadness,
The ache of your heart; this makes Me sad.

Do you think you are the only one to hurt?

In the beginning, I knew
My Son would leave Me for a period of time.

I also knew His circumstances
Would be much worse than yours.
He also knew this,
Yet We chose the same course.
We knew you would be.

I have lived in a body like yours.
I know the stress from living
In body, soul, and spirit.
I know your pain.

Allow Me to wrap Myself around you,
To flow freely within you.
I understand, I care, and I desire to help.
I desire your love much more
Than you desire Mine.

I created you
Because I wanted someone to love
And to have someone love Me.

I am love.
Allow Me to flood your being
With My love, with Me.
I was and I am My gift to you.

Sweet Child

Oh, sweet child,
I am your Father.
I love you greatly.
Yes, I care, I love, I hear, I feel.
Was it not I who gave you the feelings you have?
Then think, would not My feelings
Be much greater, deeper than yours?
I know the desires of your heart.
I will meet those desires.
You are My child.
I am your Father.
Yes, I say to you this day
I care greatly for you.
I will meet all your needs.
None of my children ever has want.
Remember, I care for all My sheep.
I am the Good Shepherd,
The good Father.
My love is deep.
Wait, child.
Do not be impatient to grow.
Growth for you is coming.
Wait.
You are young and you are new.
You are growing.
I want you to grow strong.
Read My Word.
Spend time with Me in prayer.
You will grow and you will know
I love you as you grow.
Sweet child, I love you.
Yes, I say to you, I love you.

Commitment

My daughter, now you need to persist
In the way of the Lord.
Fight back the power
Of the Enemy that has overtaken you
In your daily walk with Me.
The power of the Enemy has greatly hindered you.

If you will push forward with boldness,
I will intervene and assist you in a great and powerful victory.
Yea, my daughter, if you will persist in praise and worship,
I will move upon you and set you free.

Enter in without fear, for I am with you.
I will hold back the power of the Enemy in your life.
I will also help you to break the power
He has over your children.
I will fulfill the promises I have made to you.

This day I say that you need to enter in boldly
Without reservations.
Enter into the peace that passes all understanding

I am the Lord who delivereth thee.
My hand will be strong in your life
If you will make and keep a commitment
Unto Me this day.

Fight

Already, child, your heart grows cold.
You must keep your mind on Me at all times,
For if you don't, you could be left out.
Does not My Word say that many will come saying,
"Didn't I cast devils out in Your name?"
"Didn't I prophesy in Your name?"
"Didn't I heal the sick in Your name?"
I will say, "Depart from Me, you workers of iniquity,
For I never knew you."
Do not follow after people
Who seem to have a great following or great gifts.
Follow Me.
Many deceivers will come,
And if you are not grounded in My Word,
If you are not sure of My voice,
You will be deceived.
Many already have been deceived.
Spend time in prayer; fast and enter into praise and worship.
Then you will see Me and will learn to know Me.
When the enemy of your soul comes to you
In sheep's clothing,
You will know that he comes to steal, kill, and destroy.
Call out your need before Me and I will answer you.
I will come and heal you,
Pour My Spirit out upon you in greater measure,
And check your spirit all day and all night.
Are you ready this very second to meet your Lord?
If not, take the time right now to get ready.
Surely I come quickly.
Fight. The battle rages.

I Hear

Oh, My child, I do have ears to hear.
I feel your distress and I reach down to meet your need.
Yea, I would say to you, I have defeated the Enemy.
Seek Me through My Word
That I might bring deliverance
To you through My Word.
All who seek, find.
I am not far from you, child.
Yea, I hear all your heart's cries.
I will answer you.
I will meet your needs.
I bring healing.
I bring strength.
Discipline yourself to walk in My way, child.
Take My burden upon you and give Me yours.
Yea, I would say unto you that when you are weak
You need to turn to Me.
I will give you strength.
Yea, I will bring you strength and refreshment
In your time of need if you will turn to Me.
Yea, I desire to meet your needs.
I am the Good Shepherd.
I have pastures green
And plenty of water for your thirst.
Yea, healing is in My wings.
I will cover you with My wings,
Give you protection,
Give you sanction,
Give you peace.
Truly seek Me; I am close.
You are beloved in My sight.
I desire to meet your needs.

Looking

You were looking for My footprints.

Stand up.

You are no longer a child.
If you look behind you,
You will find My footprints
Within your own.

You are Me on the earth
When you do
The things I ask of you.

You know within yourself,
For that is where you'll find Me

Are you not My temple,
My dwelling place?

Then why look for Me
Outside of yourself?

Learn to rely on the inner witness.

Yes, it's time to stop looking for Me
And start working with Me.

You in Me,
I in you.

CAROLYN MYERS

Seek My Face

Seek My face and seek My grace.
I will find you.
Under My wing,
I will lovingly restore you.
For you have wandered far
from the protection
Of the flock.
But with My eye of love
Have I followed after you,
Gently calling to you.
You did not care to hear.
Many are the unseen wolves
I have slain for you.
Now because of your awareness
Of the fruitlessness of thy wanderings,
You desire to return to Me.
Yea, I say to you,
"Welcome home, child.
"Welcome to the love of My open arms."
The faith of thy love
Shall be restored many times over.
Yes, to a great overflowing.
Thou shall have thy love fulfilled in Me
And I in thee.
Thou shall no more wander,
For great shall thy love be to Me.
I shall sustain thee.
Seek My face.
Seek My grace.
I will find thee.

Why Do You Fret?

My child,
I am aware of your needs.

Do I not promise
I will supply all your needs?
Why do you fret?

Stand on My Word.
Hurry into the fullness of My Spirit.

I see all, for I am all.
Did I not say in My Word
That I care for My own?

Child, you are Mine.
Yea, your children are Mine.
The Enemy will not have you or yours.

I am the Good Shepherd.

Your walk will be a walk of faith,
Not of feelings.

Look to Me, not the Enemy.
Come; hide yourself in Me.

Come; eat the meat of My Spirit.
I will raise you up.

Desert Rose

Man looks at the desert
In the heat and dryness
Of its season.

He fails to see the hidden beauty
Of the dormant life there,
The desert rose.

It waits for the Master
To release the rain
That brings life.

As the rain begins to fall,
The desert drinks the rain.

Overnight the dormant seed takes root,
Springs up, and grows.

The blossom, so delicate, has strength.

The desert heat,
Fragrance sweet,
Beauty uncompared.

Yes, the desert rose shall have its season.

Make Time

Oh My child, I am your Father.
I care for you.

I will take care of you.
Entrust yourself to Me.

Lift up your heart before Me.
My hand will move for you.

I feel your hurts.
I feel your heartbreaks.

Come.
Sit at My feet.
Share your burdens with Me.

I am a good Father.

I will help with all your problems.
Seek Me, for I am near; I hear all.

Know that I am God.
I change not.

I will speak to you in a still small voice.
I am a gentle Father.

Come; sit and talk with Me.
Come this day; talk with Me.

I have time for you.
Will you make time for Me?

CAROLYN MYERS

Learning

Be not deceived, My daughter.
Your work for Me has not begun.
You are in a learning stage.
You shall learn and go forth in great power and strength
Through My Spirit.
My Word spoken through you will set many free
From the power of the Enemy.
Yea, if you obey My every leading,
You will lose your fear of man and of Satan.
Go forth in faith; do not rely on feelings.
If you do not feel Me, does it mean I am not there?
No, for I am everywhere.
You are a channel for My power.
Can you feel electrical power go through its channel, the cord?
No, but the object intended to receive it does.
Fear not to respond to Me, for if you obey
I will hold back the power of Satan from you and yours.
Pray often, telling all, keep nothing hidden.
I can work when you bring things to Me.
Yes, things will be as I have told you.
As you talk with Me, you will be less confused,
For those spirits cannot enter where you sit and talk with Me.
Sit before Me and allow Me to teach you.
I do not change My Word, and people do not repent.
If their evil hearts changed, then I would stay My hand.
They do not repent.
In some things, self stands in the way.
My answers are not heard, so speak.
You have blessed Me this day, for you praised Me
From the depth of your spirit.
As you continue to do this, you will grow.
You will grow,
For I give the increase and your heart desires to grow.
My blessings are upon you, child.

Seek Me

Seek Me; seek Me.
I am near.

Praise Me; praise Me.
I will heal

Know Me; know Me.
I am love.

Speak Me; speak Me.
I am life.

Search Me; search Me.
I am truth.

Eat Me; eat Me.
I am meat.

Know Me; know Me.
I am life

Worship Me; worship Me.
I am holy.

Seek Me; seek Me.
I am peace.

Search Me; search Me.
I AM.

Calling

Yea, My child, I am again calling you forth.
Come into My presence with the high praise
Of victory on your lips.
Come and worship Me.
Come into the fullness of joy.
Come; I am calling you forth.

Lord God, I come into Your presence,
Singing forth Your praise.
You are the Holy One.
You are the great I AM.
I worship You.

I worship You.

The Lord God is calling,
"Who will fight for Me?"
The Lord God is calling,
"Who will stand fearlessly?"
"Who is willing to do battle?
"Who will defend My cause?"
"Who? Who? Is one you?"

Hear the Lord God say,
"There is more than one way to do battle.
There is more than one strategy.
I am the God of a million possibilities.
Come; listen to My plan of action.
Come; submit yourself unto Me.
I can make you a warrior.
Will you come and do battle for Me?"

Yes, Lord, I will come.

Stand

Stand; stand firm.
Know that all I ask is
When you have done
All you can do, stand.

Stand. I will do what only I can do.
You have not seen things
As I see them,
But know I am working for you.

And your children
And all your precious grandchildren
I do not fail,
For I have overcome all things.

I sit at the right hand
Of My Father.
All things
Have been given unto Me.

Seek Me
That I may impart wisdom
And power to you.

Songs

The Shadow of His Hand

When my spirit's weary

When my body's worn

I will seek a refuge

In the shadow of His hand.

In the heat of battle

When all my strength is gone

I will seek a refuge

In the shadow of His hand.

Dear friend, the Savior's calling

All who are tired and worn.

Come sit in the refuge

In the shadow of His hand.

CAROLYN MYERS

Precious Jesus

Precious Jesus has His hand on me.
Far from His side I'll never be.

From His side I'll never stray.
His love will keep me there each day.

Though toil and strife be on all sides of me,
Jesus is the shepherd that I see.

He will calm the storm waves of my life.
Jesus, precious Jesus has His hand on me.

One day I'll see Him face to face.
All my loved ones I'll embrace.

No one could ever take His place.
Jesus, precious Jesus has His hand on me.

Chorus:

He will see me through the darkest night

For my Jesus is the very light.

Jesus, precious Jesus has His hand on me.

I Worship You

I worship You; I worship You.

You are spirit; You are truth.

I worship You.

Lord, I lay myself on Your altar

Where Your holiness burns bright.

I do not understand, but I obey.

Lord, cleanse me with Your fire.

Cause my flesh to yield.

Burn Your holiness within.

Cause me to be
Your heart's desire.
I worship You.

I worship You; I worship You.

You are spirit; You are truth.

I worship You.

CAROLYN MYERS

Servant

I am Your servant, Lord.
I am molded by Your hand.

I bow before Your throne.
I hear Your command.

"Come follow Me."

I am not ashamed
Of Your holy name.

I am Your servant, Lord.

Shine Your light of truth
On the shadows of my heart
As You impart Your life to me.

Knowing You saved me
By Your grace,
Enthralled by Your holiness,
I seek Your face.

I bow before Your throne.

"Come follow Me."

I am Your servant, Lord.
I want You to live through me.
Live through me. Live through me.
I am your servant, Lord.
Live through me.

Lord, What Have You Done?

O Lord, O Lord, what have You done?

You've gone and crucified Your Son.

You really hung Him on a tree

To reach and save a wretch like me.

O Lord, O Lord, I cannot see

The reason that You value me.

You let Him die to set me free.

You suffered much that I might see.

O Lord, O Lord, You really care.

You brought me back from sin's despair.

Through the blood of Your own Son,

You have paid the price; the victory's won.

O Lord, O Lord, I want to say

That I will help to show the way,

That in my life the world will see

The Son of God revealed in me.

Carry Me

There was a day
Not long ago
My heart was full,
I sang Your praise.
Now I'm tired
And so forlorn.
I need Your love
To carry me.

This valley's long.
I feel so dry.
I dream of mountains
Oh so high,
Of songs anew,
The battle cry.
My heart's song
Does rise to Thee.

In Your grace,
Look to me
Until at last
I am free.
My song shall ever be
You are the Lord
With mighty wings.
You carry me.

Chorus:

Carry me; carry me.
My Lord, my God,
I need You to carry me.
I praise Your love.
You carry me.

I Know Him

I can lean on Jesus.
I can lean on Jesus.
I can count on
His strong love.

Whatever befalls me,
No matter, no matter,
His love will sustain
All my needs.

I know I can trust Him.
I know I can trust Him.
I can follow
Wherever He leads.

I needn't be weary.
I needn't be weary.
I can lean on Jesus.
My burdens I've laid at His feet.

I can lean on Jesus.
I can lean on Jesus.
I can count on
His strong love.

Chorus:

I know Him,
I've tried Him,
And Jesus
He loves even me.

CAROLYN MYERS

I Love to Worship You

I love the light of Your glory.

I love the beauty of You.

I love to stand in Your presence.

Lord, I love to worship You.

I love to sing Your praises.

I love to dance for Your delight.

I love to stand in Your presence.

Lord, I love to worship You.

I love to bow before You.

I love to delight Your heart.

I love to bow in Your presence.

Lord, I love to worship You.

I worship You.

You are spirit.

You are truth.

I worship You.

Glory

Oh Jesus, my Savior,
My Lord, my Redeemer,
How beautiful You are,
Spirit living within.

I praise and adore You.
I bow down before You,
King forever to reign
In my spirit that lives.

I ever will praise You
For the things You have done.
I ever will praise You
For the liberty won.

Oh, the sacrifice, Lord,
That You gave for Your own,
Coming down from Your glory
From Your majestic throne.

To take on a body
Like mine that You wore.
Oh, the nail scars You carried
For the shame that You bore.

Forever I'm grateful
For the sacrifice made.
I'll do Your sweet bidding
Though the debt has been paid.

Oh glory, sweet Jesus,
For the work that's been done.
Oh glory forever
To the Lord for His Son.

Alive

I have been delivered.

I have been set free.

The Spirit of the living God
Is alive in me.

Walking in the power of His majesty

I have been delivered.

I have been set free.

Now I am fulfilling my destiny.

I have been delivered.

I have been set free.

Sing hallelujah.
Sing hallelujah.

Walking in the power of His majesty

I've been delivered. (echo)

I've been set free. (echo)

The Spirit of the living God
Is alive in me.

Sing hallelujah.
Sing hallelujah.
Sing hallelujah to the Lord.

Crucified

Crucified, hung upon a tree,
Cursed of God,
He could not even look at You.

Yet You were lifted up
For all the world to see.
Jesus, You died in shame for me.

Jesus Christ, Deity,
Amazing love to hang upon that tree.
Your side pierced, You died in agony.

I will never be the same.
This You did to set me free.
In all my filth, You still loved me.

Your heart's cry that I would be
Forgiven and set free.

Knowing truth, therefore I could be
A child of God to rule with Thee.

I will sing Your praise, O Majesty.

Because of Your love,
I can live in victory.

Jesus Christ, Deity,
Amazing love, You died for me.